Tell, Tale Signs of Winter!

**IN THE WINTER,
IT IS VERY COLD OUTSIDE!**

**WE NOW HAVE TO WEAR OUR BIG
COATS, HATS AND GLOVES.**

OH, AND OUR SCARVES AND BOOTS TOO!

BRRRRRR.......
TELL, TALE SIGNS OF WINTER!

MOST OF THE TREE
BRANCHES ARE BARE.

WITH NOT MUCH OF A HINT THAT LEAVES WERE EVER THERE.

GLISTENING SNOWFLAKES
FALL TO THE GROUND.

LATER, TO BE MOLDED INTO A SNOWMAN WITH BLACK BUTTONS AND A CARROT NOSE!

BRRRRRR.......
TELL, TALE SIGNS OF WINTER!

SMOKE CAN BE SEEN
RISING THROUGH CHIMNEYS,

FROM THE FIREPLACES INSIDE OF
HOMES KEEPING FAMILIES WARM.

THE CHRISTMAS HOLIDAY IS CELEBRATED WITH FAMILY AND FRIENDS.

ALONG, WITH A BEAUTIFULLY DECORATED CHRISTMAS TREE AND PRESENTS UNDERNEATH.

BRRRRRR.......
Tell, Tale Signs of Winter!

HOT COCOA WITH SPONGY MARSHMALLOWS IS DELICIOUS IN THE WINTERTIME.

AS THE GRAY SKIES HOVER OVER US, FROM TIME TO TIME.

SOMETIMES, BECAUSE IT'S SO COLD
THE RAIN DROPS FREEZES.

WE CALL THAT FREEZING RAIN.

BUT, DURING THIS COLD SEASON VALENTINE'S DAY WARMS OUR HEARTS WITH LOVE.

BRRRRRR.......
TELL, TALE SIGNS OF WINTER!

REMEMBER, THE WINTER SEASON IS VERY COLD; BUT, STAYING WARM NEVER GETS OLD!